AN IDEAS INTO ACTION GUIDEBOOK

IDEAS INTO ACTION GUIDEBOOKS

Aimed at managers and executives who are concerned with their own and others' development, each guidebook in this series gives specific advice on how to complete a developmental task or solve a leadership problem.

LEAD CONTRIBUTOR	Dennis Lindoerfer
CONTRIBUTORS	Vidula Bal
	David Gonzalez
	Douglas Ryden
DIRECTOR OF PUBLICATIONS	Martin Wilcox
EDITOR	Peter Scisco
ASSOCIATE EDITOR	Karen Lewis
DESIGN AND LAYOUT	Joanne Ferguson
CONTRIBUTING ARTISTS	Laura J. Gibson
	Chris Wilson, 29 & Company

CCL No. 437
ISBN No. 978-1-60491-021-6

CENTER FOR CREATIVE LEADERSHIP
POST OFFICE BOX 26300
GREENSBORO, NORTH CAROLINA 27438-6300
336-288-7210
WWW.CCL.ORG / PUBLICATIONS

AN IDEAS INTO ACTION GUIDEBOOK

Raising Sensitive Issues In a Team

Dennis Lindoerfer

Center for Creative Leadership

NORTH AMERICA EUROPE ASIA

www.ccl.org

THE IDEAS INTO ACTION GUIDEBOOK SERIES

This series of guidebooks draws on the practical knowledge that the Center for Creative Leadership (CCL®) has generated, since its inception in 1970, through its research and educational activity conducted in partnership with hundreds of thousands of managers and executives. Much of this knowledge is shared—in a way that is distinct from the typical university department, professional association, or consultancy. CCL is not simply a collection of individual experts, although the individual credentials of its staff are impressive; rather it is a community, with its members holding certain principles in common and working together to understand and generate practical responses to today's leadership and organizational challenges.

The purpose of the series is to provide managers with specific advice on how to complete a developmental task or solve a leadership challenge. In doing that, the series carries out CCL's mission to advance the understanding, practice, and development of leadership for the benefit of society worldwide. We think you will find the Ideas Into Action Guidebooks an important addition to your leadership toolkit.

Table of Contents

EXECUTIVE BRIEF

Many things have potential to become sensitive issues in team situations. The issue could be something that is happening outside the awareness of most of the team members or something that results from marked differences between them. It may serve to avoid conflict, involve embarrassing human foibles, run counter to prevailing cultural expectations, or go against espoused team norms. This guidebook focuses on ways to determine whether to raise such an issue in a team meeting—and if so, how.

From Awareness to Intervention

Have you ever wondered how to deal with a sensitive issue within your team? For example, how do you raise the issue that the women on your team rarely get listened to? How do you bring up your observation that the team members from Marketing always dominate the airwaves in team meetings? How do you talk about the fact that team teleconferences are always scheduled at times convenient for the team members in the company's headquarters in Paris? How do you talk about the fact that the women on the team exchange knowing glances every time one of the men makes a remark with thinly veiled sexual content? How do you mention that the team seems to be caught in groupthink, agreeing to poorly conceived decisions for the sake of team harmony?

This guidebook focuses on ways to bring up a touchy or sensitive issue in a team meeting. As is obvious from the limited sample just listed, there is a huge array of issues that may be sensitive in any particular team at any given point in time. Any number of things can make such issues touchy. They may be processes that are happening outside the awareness of most of the members of the team, processes that result from some of the marked differences between the team members, processes that serve to avoid conflict between team members, processes that involve embarrassing human foibles, processes that run counter to prevailing cultural expectations, or processes that are contrary to espoused team norms.

We're going to examine the evolution of an intervention about a sensitive team issue by a team member—possibly the team's leader.

1. The intervention begins with a fledgling awareness that something of some relevance to the team's functioning is occurring.

2. The team member then begins to focus more closely on what he or she has noticed, making some assessment of its nature and observing its impact on himself or herself, other team members, and the team at large.

3. The team member at some point makes the judgment that what is happening (a) is not a relevant issue for him or her, other team members, or the team; (b) helps him or her, other team members, and the team's functioning and needs to be pointed out and encouraged; or (c) hinders him or her, other team members, or the team's functioning and needs to be pointed out and remedied.

4. Depending on the judgment made at this juncture, he or she decides whether to act on the issue or not—to borrow from poker jargon, to raise or to hold.

We'll look at this process in more detail; talk a bit about self, others, and team assessment; and explore the judgment juncture of raise versus hold.

Elements of the Process

The scenario on page 9 captures several core elements of the process we're exploring. The first element is an awareness of what is transpiring. We use our awareness of our own thoughts, feelings, and behaviors during a meeting of a team to monitor the progression of events. Our reactions in these domains lead us to conclude

Scenario 1

A team member sitting in a team meeting notices that he is having a hard time getting the opportunity to get his thoughts about the work aired. He recollects that this is more often than not the case in the last few meetings. He begins to pay a bit more attention to which of the team members are doing the most talking and which ones are saying little or nothing.

Over the next half hour of the meeting, he notices that the marketing director (a white male with considerable seniority in the company), an information technology manager (a white male, new to the company but quite senior and previously from a competitor), and the manufacturing director (the team's nominal leader, a white male who has come up through the ranks over his career) are dominating the conversation. The other five team members are saying little or nothing.

He's pretty sure that some version of this pattern has been prevalent for the last few team meetings, and he suspects that the three big talkers have joined together in a subgroup of the team to push their shared agenda for the project. They happen to be the only males on the team who are white and the only team members with substantial seniority in their specialties.

He struggles with the judgment about whether this emerging communication pattern is good or bad for the team's functioning. It makes some sense that these experienced members with considerable credibility are influencing the nature of the team's work. Yet the relative lack of involvement of himself and the four other team members seems to be blocking the team's customary operating style and the free-flowing exchange of ideas.

He reaches the judgment that what he's seeing is a problem at least for him and may be a problem for other members of the team and the team as a whole. He decides to bring the issue up, so he finds an opportunity in the discussion and raises the issue.

that things are going well or not so well. Our awareness of the behavior, both verbal and nonverbal, of our teammates and our speculation about the thoughts and feelings these behaviors are tied to are other sources of information we observe and process to evaluate the team's functioning.

The first element is an awareness of what is transpiring.

We also maintain some awareness of how our team is working. Most of our teams have goals established and interim milestones set, and we team members are continually or periodically checking these to see whether the team is making progress. Team maintenance and team learning goals, in addition to the more task-focused goals set by the organization, are particularly useful in this regard. These metrics help us determine whether or not our team is working effectively, both at the moment and over time.

Additionally, conceptual and experience-based frameworks that all of us have accumulated during our working lives provide us with benchmarks against which we measure how our team is working. These frameworks create expectations for how things should go when we work with others in teams.

The point of this is that we have available to us, at any given time in a team's working life, numerous sources of data we can use to stimulate our awareness of when things are working and when they're not. (Read and consider the indicators on page 11 to increase your own awareness.) We have to attend to this data, make some sense out of it, and then decide what, if anything, to do about it.

Reading the Signs

Leader thoughts indicating poor teamwork:
- This conversation is going nowhere.
- I'm confused.
- These people are working at cross purposes.
- This isn't working the way I hoped it would.
- These people aren't taking direction from me.
- This isn't where I thought we would be at this point.

Leader behaviors indicating poor teamwork:
- I continually redirect the conversation.
- I take on tasks team members should be doing.
- I offer to reset deadlines and milestones.
- I offer to request more resources or budget.
- I end meetings early.
- I cancel meetings.
- I conduct meetings after the official meetings.
- I change the subject when things get tense.

Team behaviors indicating task distress:
- The team misses deadlines.
- The team repeats the same mistakes over and over again.
- The team is continually resetting milestones.
- The team members do something other than what they say they'll do.
- The subteams fail to deliver their parts.

Team behaviors indicating relational distress:
- Unresolved issues continue to resurface.
- People don't come to meetings or don't participate.
- People are otherwise engaged during meetings.
- People quibble over minor issues.
- People take potshots at the leader or each other.
- People use lots of sarcasm.
- Comments don't build on previous comments.
- There is obvious animosity between subgroups.

In the scenario on page 9, the team member first noticed some frustration he was feeling in a team meeting. He then recollected that he'd been feeling the same type of frustration for several team meetings. He decided to watch the communication in the team more closely for a bit of time. When he saw the pattern that emerged, he developed a judgment about whether the pattern was helping or hindering himself, other team members, and the team. He used whatever knowledge, prior experience, mental models, and expectations he possessed to make this judgment.

This is a difficult judgment and more art than science. There is no set formula. You have to weigh what you see happening against your ideas and expectations about what should or might be happening. Whether you determine that what you're experiencing is helping the team or hindering it, you still must decide whether to raise or to hold.

Raise or Hold

There are times to leave it be—that is, to hold. For example, you're pretty sure that what you're picking up on isn't good for the team, but it seems to be resolving itself as the team works. Or perhaps some change in the team or its work is about to occur and you think that change will break up the dysfunctional process you're concerned about. You should also hold when you need to gather more information. Perhaps you're unsure of what it is that you're reacting to, you don't know whether what you're seeing in the team is a good thing or a bad thing, it's unclear how others are responding to what's happening or whether they're even noticing, or you think that what's happening is only a transient or situational occurrence and need to wait and see.

Then there are times to take it forward—that is, to raise. For example, you're convinced that what's happening is a clear problem for you, other team members, or the team's effectiveness. Or maybe what you're picking up on doesn't seem to be too much of a problem right now, but it's obviously getting worse. Or it may be clear that the team's current way of working will become an even bigger problem in the next phase of the work. The team may have an active norm of full disclosure about things the members become aware of, or it may have the goal of becoming a high-performance team.

By the way, the process we're exploring here applies equally to team leaders and team members. However, team leaders carry more responsibility for monitoring and raising issues, especially in the early life of a team. Establishing an atmosphere in a team where members are paying attention to what's going on, assessing what they see happening in a thoughtful way, and talking about their assessments in an open, exploratory fashion will do more to help a team reach high performance than almost any other team process.

On the Flip Side

You may determine that the dynamic you're picking up on is actually a good thing. Maybe it's helpful to you, to other team members, or to the team's functioning as a whole. Perhaps you're certain that the team will become even more effective if it operates more often in the way you are noticing. Of course, it's possible that the positive thing you're seeing is so obvious to everyone that you'll look naïve if you mention it. If that doesn't appear to be a concern, you should point out the dynamic in order to encourage it.

How to Raise

Let's assume you've decided to raise a sensitive, touchy issue in your team. To review how you arrived at this point, you picked up on a pattern in the team's functioning, decided that this pattern is interfering with your or other team members' effective contribution to the team or the team's effective functioning, and made the decision to bring the issue to the team's attention. Your goal is to get the team to explore the issue for its impact and decide what to do based on this exploration. How can you raise the issue in a way that is most likely to accomplish this goal?

A couple of the fundamentals of basic human relations are good initial guidelines here. First, talk about yourself: your thoughts, your feelings, your behavior. Make "I" statements: I'm thinking, I'm feeling, I'm doing. Self-disclosing your own reactions to what's happening is always the safest way to begin wading into potentially troubled waters. It models directness and openness, and is less likely to elicit defensiveness in the other team members. Second, avoid using pejorative, inflammatory terms; judgmental labels; and sweeping generalizations. Such trigger words or phrases flare team members' defensiveness and make it hard for them to respond effectively to your comments. Before speaking your mind, consider and make decisions about several other factors.

Level of Focus

One factor to consider is the level of focus of your intervention. At all times in a team meeting, things are going on within the individual members, between the members, and at the whole team level simultaneously. As interactions occur, the individual

14

members have their own internal thoughts and feelings about these interactions, the various relationships between the members are affected by these same interactions, and the team's methods of operating are either being reinforced or altered.

Your goal is to get the team to explore the issue for its impact and decide what to do based on this exploration.

When you comment on some aspect of what you are experiencing in the team, decide which level of these simultaneous processes you will focus on. You might make an individually focused intervention: "Bob, I've noticed that you interrupt other people frequently, and it makes me uncomfortable." You might make an interpersonally focused intervention: "Sarah and Janice, I'm concerned with how upset you two seem to be with each other." You might make a team-focused intervention: "I think we're being really critical of each other in this meeting, and that's making me less inclined to participate."

There are at least two strategies for making a decision about level of focus. One is the "deep end of the pool" approach. Intervene where you think the action is the hottest. If the whole team is blissfully caught up in groupthink—supporting, reinforcing, and agreeing with each other, while sacrificing in-depth examination of the issues—jump into the deep end of the pool and say something like "I think we're sacrificing the quality of our decisions for the sake of getting along, and it makes me uncomfortable." If you think two members of the team are nurturing an unresolved conflict between them and using this to avoid dealing with each other directly, say something like "Erin and Mike, I'm noticing that you two haven't said one word to each other during the whole meeting, and I'm wondering what's up with that." If you think one member of the team is dominating the discussion with his loudness and excessive verbiage, say something like "Stan, it seems to me that we've been hearing mostly about your ideas on this issue, and I'd like to hear some of the thinking of some of the rest of the team." This type of direct approach is likely to get the issue recognized and the discussion going, but it can't be carried off comfortably by everyone, nor in every circumstance by anyone.

A second strategy is to focus where the action is less hot, the "shallow end of the pool." Once you have the other team members in the water with you, you can begin to herd them up into the deeper water. For example, in the groupthink situation mentioned a moment ago, rather than confront the whole team about this team level issue, you might focus at the individual level and say, "Jane, I've seen you start to say something a couple of times but then stop, and I'm wondering whether you have a different perspective on the issue we're talking about." In the situation where two members are seemingly holding a grudge and avoiding dealing with each other, you might focus at the team level rather than the interpersonal level and say, "I think we need to revisit our team norm about how we handle conflicts between us. Our norm about not letting disagreements get personal isn't working." In the situation where one of the team members is monopolizing the conversation, you might focus at the team level rather than the individual level and say, "One of our norms in this team is to make sure everyone gets heard on a particular issue, yet that obviously is not how we are operating at the moment." The "shallow end of the pool" strategy approaches the core issue in a more tangential fashion, but when followed through with, this approach can also be very effective.

Degree of Intensity

Another factor to be thoughtful and decisional about before raising a sensitive issue in a team is the degree of intensity you want to build into your intervention. The general rule here is to use only as much intensity as it takes to get the team to explore the issue.

Low-intensity interventions usually take the form of carefully worded statements. These may sound like "It seems to me that our team teleconferences are usually scheduled during normal business hours at headquarters" or "I'm feeling pretty frustrated with how much off-task horseplay we're doing in this meeting" or "I'm irritated by the fact that nobody seems to pay much attention to my comments." Such interventions declare an issue to see how the team responds.

A moderate-intensity intervention usually consists of an observation followed by a question. This may sound something like "I'm noticing that the opinions of the women in here don't seem to get the same thoughtful consideration as the opinions of the men. Has anyone else noticed this?" or "It seems that most of our meeting time is spent discussing Marketing's issues. Is this, in fact, the best use of our time together?" or "It seems to me we're taking an approach that has minimizing risk as its major benefit. Will this really get us where we need to be in the marketplace?" Such interventions declare an issue and press the team to respond to it.

High-intensity interventions really put the pressure on. They usually consist of an observation and an interpretation of the cause of the pattern observed. High-intensity interventions sound like "I've noticed a number of times that when Allen makes an off-color remark, Sandy and Mia exchange knowing, irritated glances with each other. I'm guessing that's because you two share some feelings about this kind of behavior, and I'd like to hear what they are" or "Richard and Sydney, I've noticed that neither of you has so much as looked at the other since this meeting began. I'm guessing that's because there are still some angry feelings between you from the exchange you had in the last meeting, and I'd like to check that out and see if we can get it resolved" or "I believe this team is way behind the power curve in terms of the likelihood of meeting our deadline for this project, and I think that's because we aren't all committed to what we're doing here."

Use only as much intensity as it takes to get the team to explore the issue.

High-intensity interventions declare an issue and pose a possible explanation for the issue's existence. They are high intensity because they label the action with an interpretation of the underlying dynamics. Their directness can be shocking to the team members, and interpretations of the team's (or members') behavior increase the tension in the team. Such interventions, though potentially potent, are risky. The interpretation offered may be wrong, and if it is, the team may easily dismiss the intervention without examining the issue for a more accurate understanding. The interpretation may be accurate, but the team may attack the interpretation and/or its author and use this diversion to avoid facing the issue the intervention was targeting.

So back to our guideline. Use only the degree of intensity that is necessary to get your intervention to stick. What happens if you use too little intensity? The team ignores your comments and wonders why you're distracting them with meaningless commentary. What happens if you use too much intensity? The team members defensively band together and consider you the issue on the table rather than the team dynamic you were trying to highlight.

In practice, it's good to start with low-intensity interventions and then ratchet up the intensity until you get the response from the team you are looking for. There are some wide differences in terms of people's preferences about the intensity and level of interventions. Some people are most comfortable with low-intensity team interventions, others are most comfortable with high-intensity interpersonal interventions, and so on. The point here is that regardless of the type of intervention you are most comfortable with, you need to be able to effectively use all combinations so you can match your choices to the contextual demands in the team at the time you are intervening.

Timing

The final factor to make a good judgment about before raising a sensitive issue in a team is timing. Your goal is to get your observation listened to and given thoughtful consideration by the team, so you need to make a determination about the best circumstances in which to make your point. There is no "right" answer here, and intuition and interpersonal skill are required. In some circumstances (when the dynamic is, in your judgment, particularly problematic, or when the dynamic is subtle or complicated), you will be more effective stopping the action and bringing it up while you see the team caught up in it. In other circumstances (when the dynamic is not particularly problematic, or when you think the key parties to the dynamic will respond so defensively that no useful exploration will occur), you will more likely be effective bringing the issue up when the team is not currently playing it out. There are no clear-cut guidelines here, just some things to be attuned to and a judgment to be made.

Once you've noticed a dynamic that is likely to be sensitive operating in your team, and you've decided to bring it up, make a judgment about content level, intensity, and timing; focus on your own reactions; avoid inflammatory language; and go for it. Chances are that others on the team are having some similar observations and reactions, and will eventually come out of the woodwork to support your efforts.

Intervention by a Team Leader

Another scenario (page 21) involves a team that doesn't want to discuss an issue. They don't want to go there. Their reluctance to talk about what is happening with this dynamic is a testament to its sensitivity (that is, scariness), and you have to decide what course of action to take. Let's explore ways to face this team challenge.

Actually, your position is not all that different from that of a team member who has picked up on a dynamic operating in the team and is trying various methods of getting that dynamic talked about. As the leader, though, you'll likely be feeling a bit more pressure about this than your typical team member may feel. You may even be wondering if your lack of success in getting this dynamic explored is undermining your authority and credibility in the team.

Scenario 2

You've made a couple of attempts to get your team to recognize and talk about the fact that the two team members from the company's headquarters in Germany are never challenged or even questioned when they make a declarative statement about some aspect of the team's work. It's clear to you, as the team leader, that the rest of the team is giving these two way too much unofficial authority to shape this project, and you are concerned that this dynamic will lead to a suboptimal final work product.

You've tried to model, from time to time, a questioning, exploring response to comments from each of them. When others on the team have looked confused or annoyed while one of these two members is talking, you've directly asked those others to talk about what's on their minds. You've used a couple of opportunities to review the team norms around open engagement and productive debate. You've even raised the issue directly by saying, "You know, it seems to me that when Hugo and Marta talk in here, their words carry more weight than anyone else's, and I'm wondering what that might be about." Your team members' reaction? Nothing! Nichts! Nada! Rien! What do you do?

Whether to Raise It

It's a good idea to have a pretty clear idea about what some of the reasons might be behind the reluctance on the team's part to face the issue at hand. There is a virtually limitless array of dynamic processes that may be in play, ranging from the fact that Hugo and Marta report directly to the CEO at headquarters and aren't trusted by the other team members to the team's customary passivity in the face of any show of authority or force. You have to use your powers of observation, your prior team experience, your awareness of the personalities of the team members, and your knowledge of team dynamics to develop ideas about the possible issues in play. Depending on your confidence in your interpretations, your judgment about the degree of helpfulness or harmfulness of the pattern you are seeing, and your goals and expectations for the team, you have alternatives to choose from.

Assessing these three areas as clearly as you can will put you in a good position to decide what to do. The clearer the hunch you have about what's feeding what you're seeing, the more helpful or harmful you think what you're seeing is, and the higher your goals and expectations for the team, the more motivation you'll likely experience for hitting the issue head on. The murkier the hunch, the more uncertain your judgment about helpfulness or harmfulness, and the lower your goals and expectations for the team, the less motivation you will likely feel, and the more likely you will be to let things roll for a bit to see what develops. You're basically deciding whether to force the issue onto the table or let it ride for a while to see whether the dynamic will build to the point where it will clarify and become more difficult for the team to ignore.

How to Raise It

For our purposes here, we're looking at how you raise something when you've decided to do so. If you've made the choice to let things ride, the dynamic process you've been observing will either resolve on its own, continue, or build. The latter two outcomes will likely bring you back to this point of pushing for open examination of the issue at a later time.

So you're going to raise it. To do so, you can use what we've covered earlier. You can change the level of focus of your intervention, step up the intensity of your intervention, or both.

If you've been making interventions at the team level ("I'd like to hear from everyone before we move on"), you might switch to the interpersonal level ("Bob, it seems that you and Marta share a lot of similar ideas about this part of our work") or the individual level ("Sandy, I noticed when Hugo made that point so emphatically, you looked down at your papers and began to fidget. What was going on with you at that point?"). If you've mostly been intervening at the interpersonal level, try moving to the team level or the individual level. If you were at the individual level, try moving to the interpersonal level or the team level.

In making this shift, you're searching for a perspective on what's happening in the team from which members are willing to begin to talk about the dynamic in question.

You step up the intensity of your interventions by front-loading them with more disclosure of your observations, your thoughts and feelings, and your interpretations about the dynamic that is concerning you. You're doing this to increase the pressure on the team to talk directly about what's going on.

If you've been making exploratory interventions consisting of open-ended questions ("I'm wondering how everyone is feeling about the decision we just made"), put a little more heat in the mix by adding an observation ("A couple of you don't look as if you have your heart in this decision. What's going on?"), your own thoughts and/or feelings ("I think we didn't examine this issue in enough detail before we piled on in the direction Marta and Hugo seemed to be headed. What do the rest of you think?"), or your interpretation of the dynamic ("It seems to me that this team is giving Marta and Hugo a lot of clout in shaping our work because they seem to be wired into headquarters. Does it seem that way to others too?").

The Process in Brief

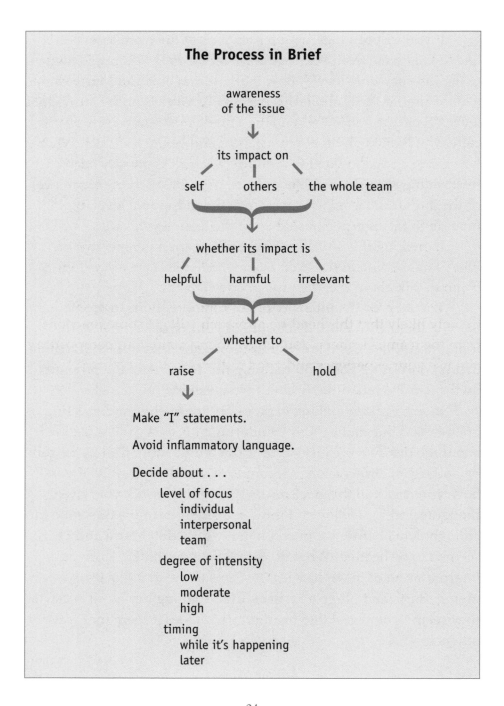

awareness
of the issue

↓

its impact on

self   others   the whole team

↓

whether its impact is

helpful   harmful   irrelevant

↓

whether to

raise   hold

↓

Make "I" statements.

Avoid inflammatory language.

Decide about . . .

    level of focus
        individual
        interpersonal
        team

    degree of intensity
        low
        moderate
        high

    timing
        while it's happening
        later

If you still can't get team members to start to explore the dynamic you see happening, you may have to be more direct or even blunt ("I think Marta and Hugo are dominating our work together, and I don't think that's ultimately going to serve our team well. Let's talk about this"). You might even bring up the fact that you've been trying to get the team to address this issue for some time without any apparent impact. This latter approach focuses directly on you and the team dynamics about your leadership authority and effectiveness.

In such a case, you may say something like "I've been trying for the last thirty minutes to get us to talk about Marta and Hugo's dominating our discussion about the licensing agreements, and none of you have been willing to address it. I'm frustrated at your willingness to ignore my attempts to lead this team." It is extremely likely that this head-on approach will get some reactions from the team members. You'll have to maintain your composure and use your experience and good judgment to work through these reactions to an effective resolution. Again, there is no prescription or formula here. You have to deal with what you face. Such interventions, when worked through to an effective resolution, can dramatically raise the performance of a team.

As stated earlier, use only the level of intensity it takes to get the problematic issue talked about. If you use too little, the team will ignore you. If you use too much, the team will likely attack you. Most savvy team leaders ratchet up the intensity of their interventions gradually, so as to avoid overplaying their hands. Of course, you can use a combination of level shifting and intensity increasing, if you're clever and experienced enough to manage that much complexity.

Stimulation ... and Terror

Getting a team to explore a sensitive issue they may not be aware of, or may be aware of but don't want to look at, is a daunting task for both team leaders and team members. Take some comfort in the fact that you can usually count on at least one other team member to have some glimmering recognition of the issue you're trying to raise and to join in on the side of full exploration and resolution once the issue is surfaced. Such critical interactions epitomize the stimulation and terror of leading teams.

Suggested Readings

Earley, P. C., & Gibson, C. B. (2002). *Multinational work teams: A new perspective.* London: Lawrence Erlbaum Associates.

Hackman, J. R. (2002). *Leading teams: Setting the stage for great performances.* Boston: Harvard Business School Press.

Kanaga, K., & Browning, H. (2003). *Maintaining team performance.* Greensboro, NC: Center for Creative Leadership.

Kossler, M. E., & Prestridge, S. (2004). *Leading dispersed teams.* Greensboro, NC: Center for Creative Leadership.

Runde, C. E., & Flanagan, T. A. (2008). *Building conflict competent teams.* San Francisco: Jossey-Bass.

Thompson, L. L. (2003). *Making the team: A guide for managers* (2nd ed.). Upper Saddle River, NJ: Prentice Hall.

Wheelan, S. A. (2005). *Creating effective teams: A guide for members and leaders.* Thousand Oaks, CA: Sage Publications.

Background

Since 1990, the Center for Creative Leadership (CCL) has worked with many organizations and teams through its educational initiatives. The goal of these initiatives is to help participants develop team management skills through experience with practical team-oriented applications. These developmental experiences provide research-based information about how high-performance teams work. They cover such areas as team member selection, cross-cultural differences in teams, and resolving team conflict.

CCL continues to develop its understanding of teams—how they can be led more effectively, how they can best achieve organizational goals, and how they can be created and maintained for improved results. Its goal is to pass that understanding on to team leaders and their organizations so that teams can meet and even surpass performance expectations.

Key Point Summary

In your role as a team member or leader, there may be times when you need to bring up sensitive issues within the team. You begin with an awareness that something of some relevance to the team's functioning is occurring. You assess what you have noticed and observe its impact on yourself, other team members, and the team at large. You decide whether the dynamic is helpful, harmful, or not relevant after all. Depending on this decision, you determine whether or not to act on the issue—to raise or to hold.

If you decide to raise, the following guidelines may be helpful: Make "I" statements. Avoid inflammatory language. Consider and make decisions about level of focus, degree of intensity, and timing.

The level of focus can be individual, interpersonal, or team. Two strategies for making a decision about level of focus are the "deep end of the pool" and the "shallow end of the pool." That is, you choose to approach the issue directly or indirectly.

For degree of intensity, the general rule is to use only as much intensity as it takes to get the team to explore the issue. It's good to start with low-intensity interventions and then ratchet up the intensity if necessary.

The final factor is timing. In some circumstances, you will be more effective stopping the action and bringing up the issue while the team is caught up in it. In other circumstances, it will be better to bring it up when the team is not currently playing it out.

Once you've decided to bring up a sensitive issue, focus on your own reactions; avoid inflammatory language; make a judgment about level of focus, degree of intensity, and timing; and then go for it. Chances are that others on the team have similar observations and reactions.